THE WORSHIP PIANO METHOD

Songbook

LEVEL 1

To access audio visit:
www.halleonard.com/mylibrary

Enter Code
8572-1073-2044-7271

ISBN 978-1-4803-9457-5

7777 W. BLUEMOUND RD. P.O. BOX 13819 MILWAUKEE, WI 53213

Visit Hal Leonard Online at
www.halleonard.com

There Is a Redeemer

Words and Music by
Melody Green

Thankfully ♩ = 144

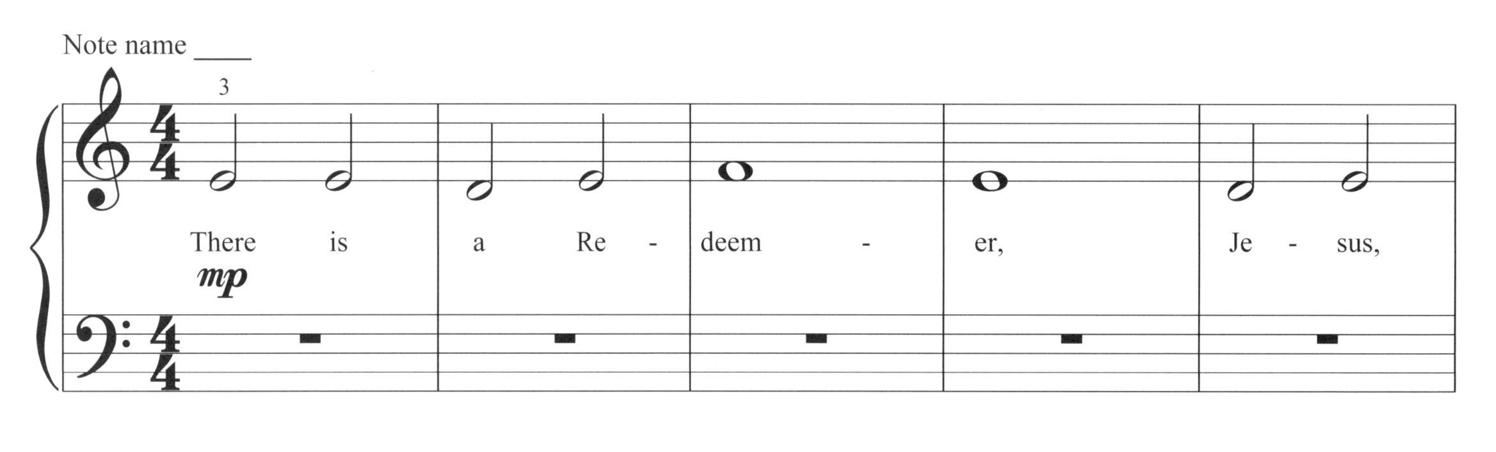

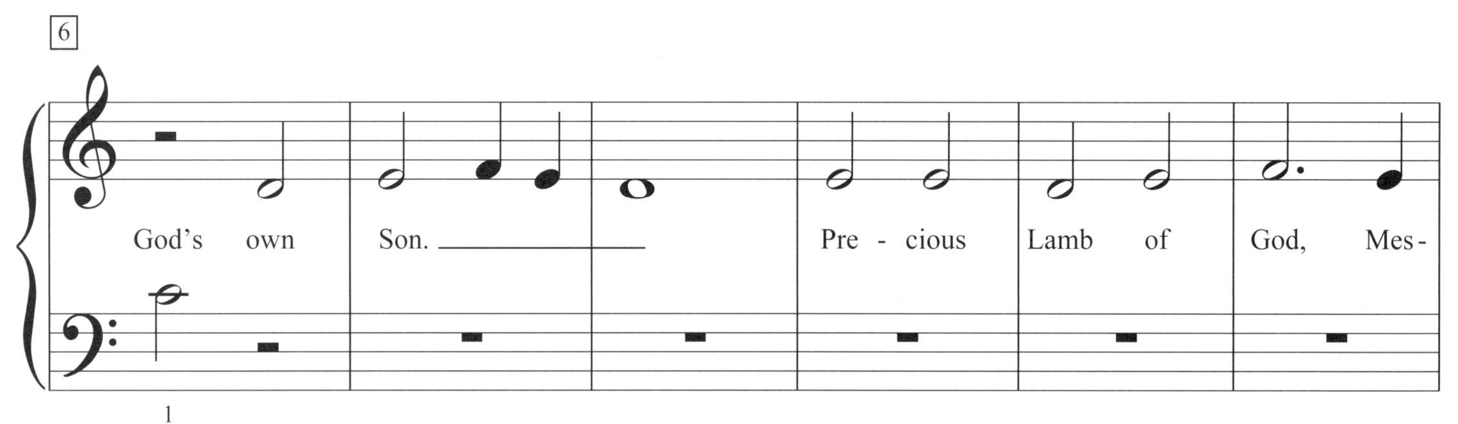

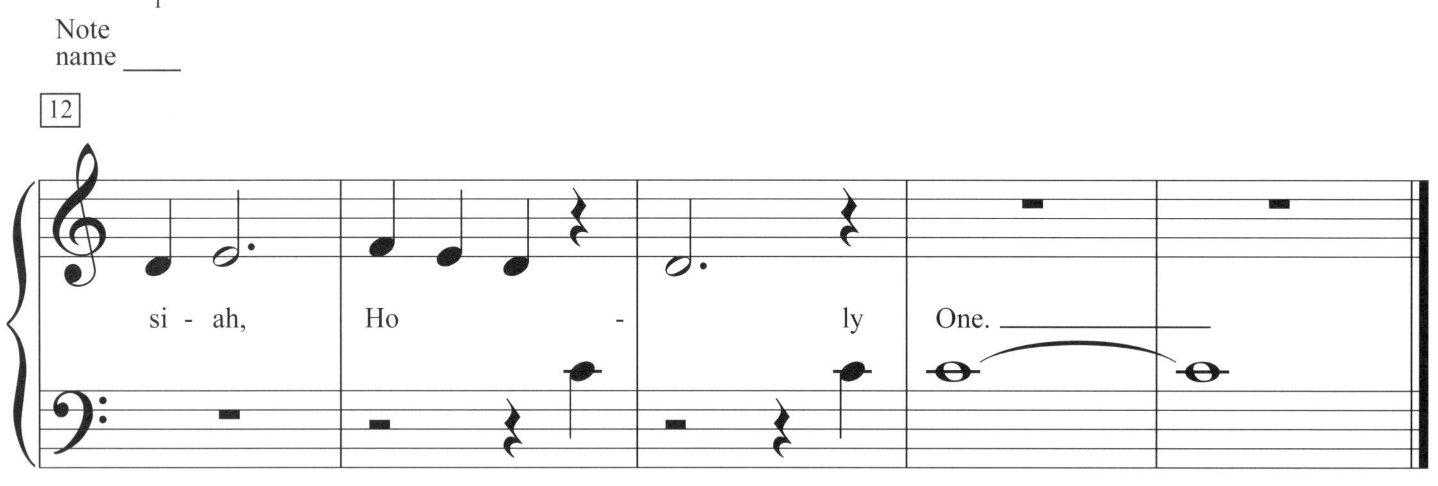

Accompaniment (Student plays one octave higher than written.)

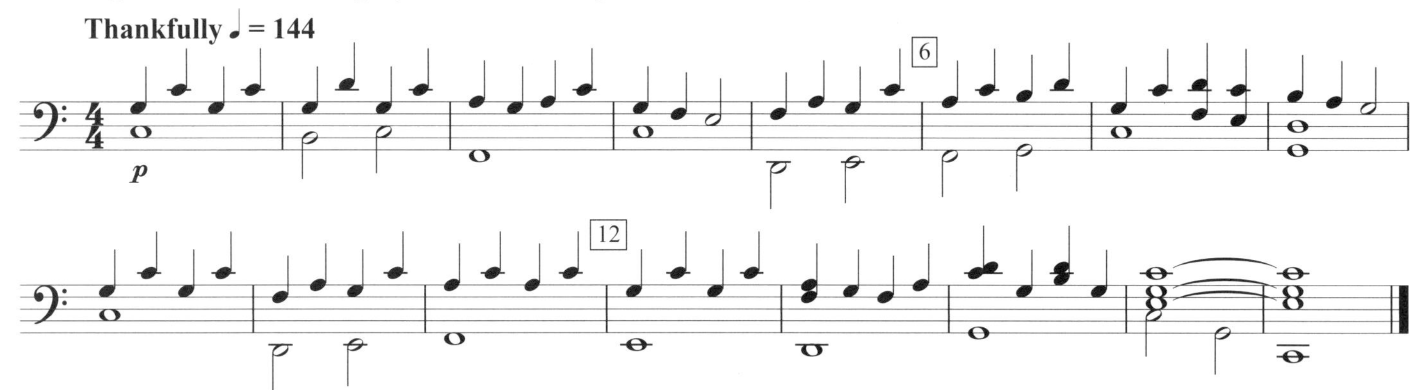

Seek Ye First

(Matthew 6:33)

Words and Music by
Karen Lafferty

With confidence ♩ = 136

Accompaniment (Student plays one octave higher than written.)

With confidence ♩ = 136

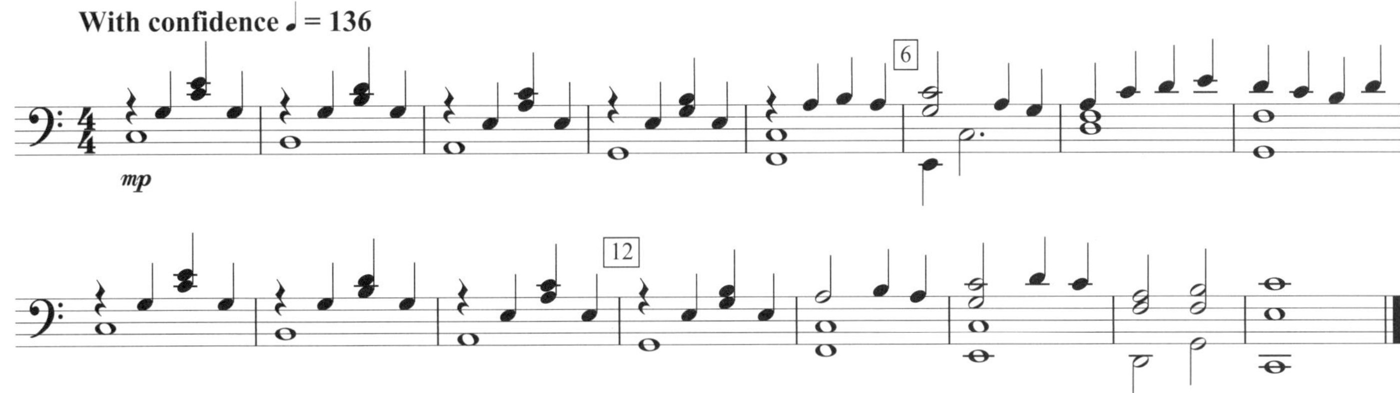

Oh Lord, You're Beautiful

Words and Music by
Keith Green

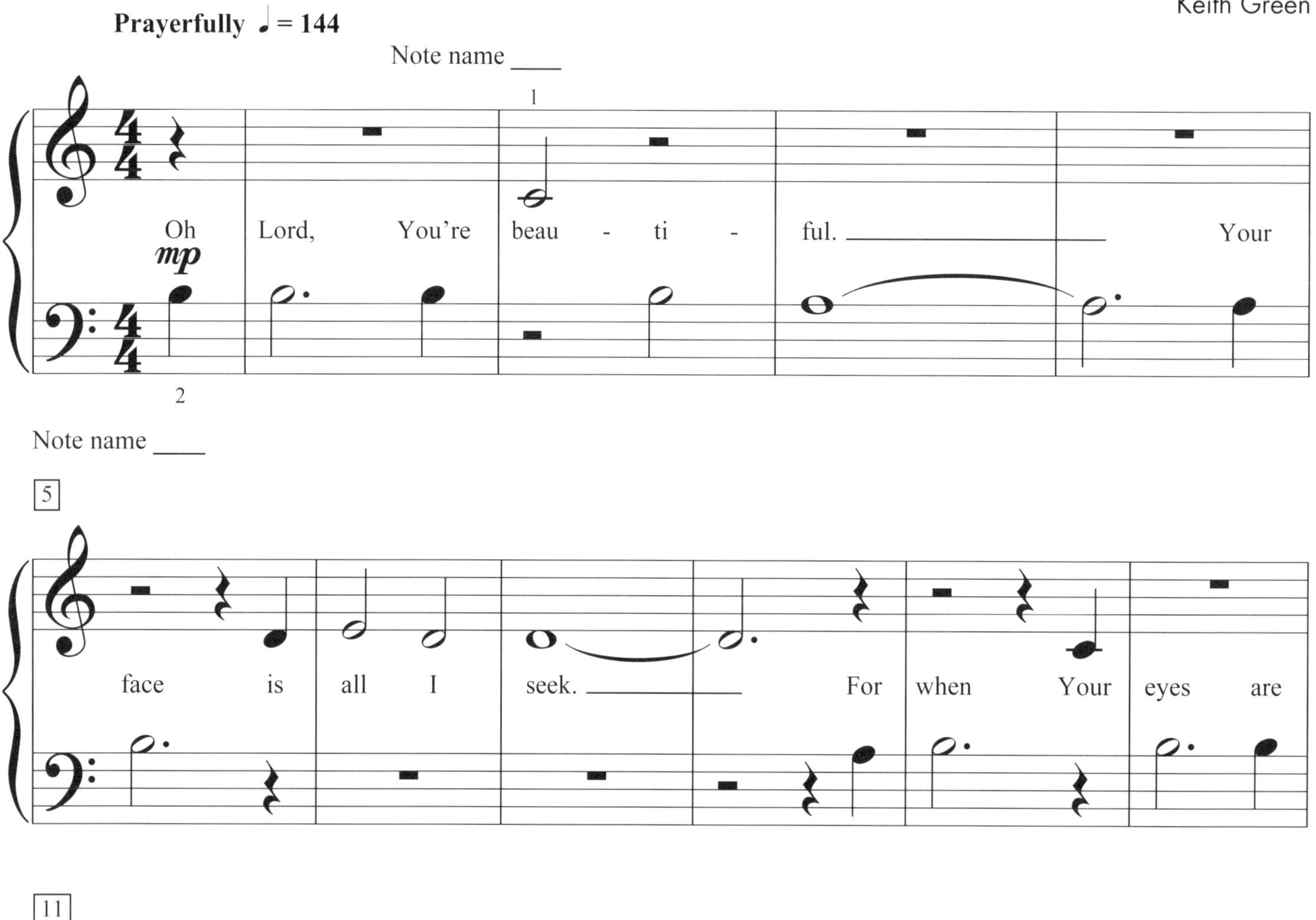

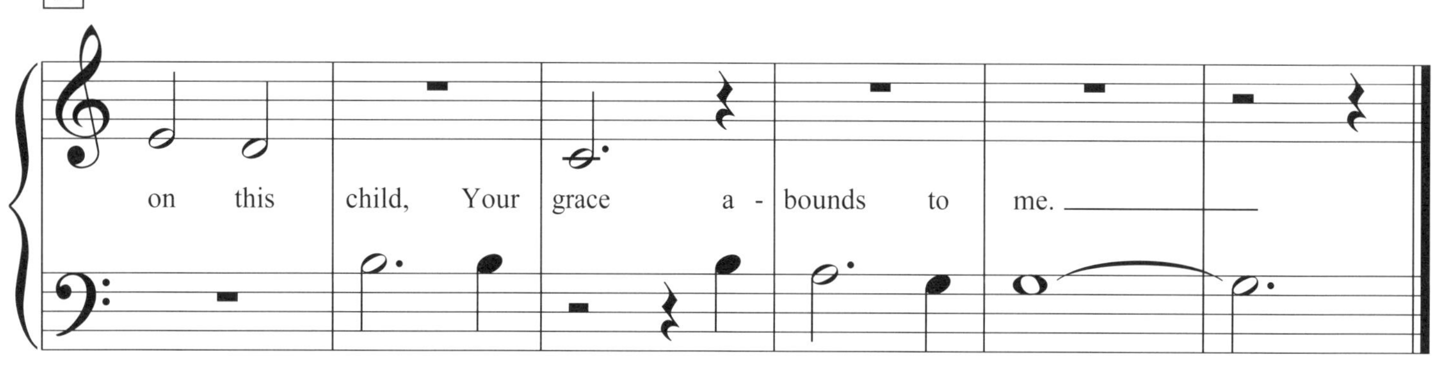

Accompaniment (Student plays one octave higher than written.)

"God, Your ways are holy.
No god is as great as our God."
– Psalm 77:13, NCV®

How Great Is Our God

Words and Music by Chris Tomlin,
Jesse Reeves and Ed Cash

Worshipfully ♩ = 160

Accompaniment (Student plays one octave higher than written.)

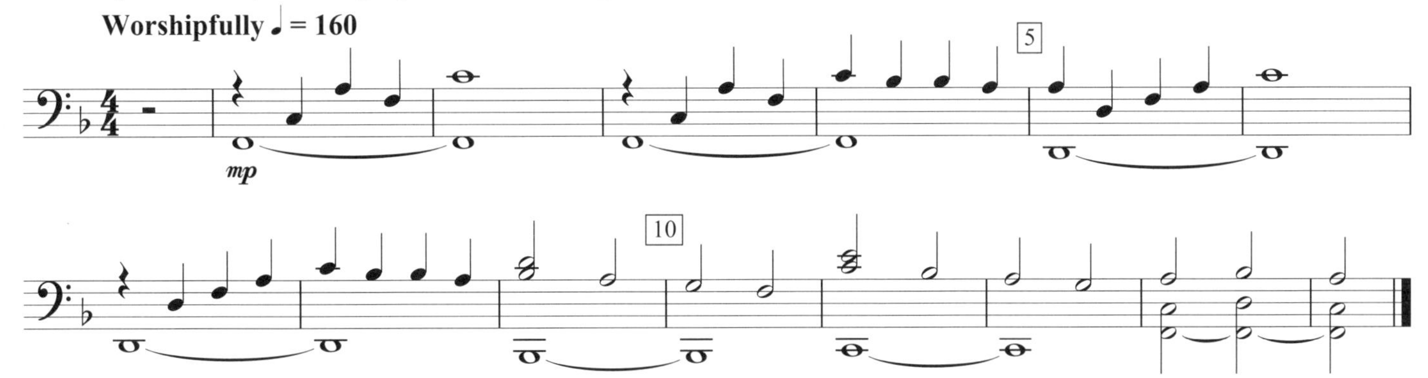

I Will Call Upon the Lord

(Psalm 18:3)

Words and Music by
Michael O'Shields

Note name ____

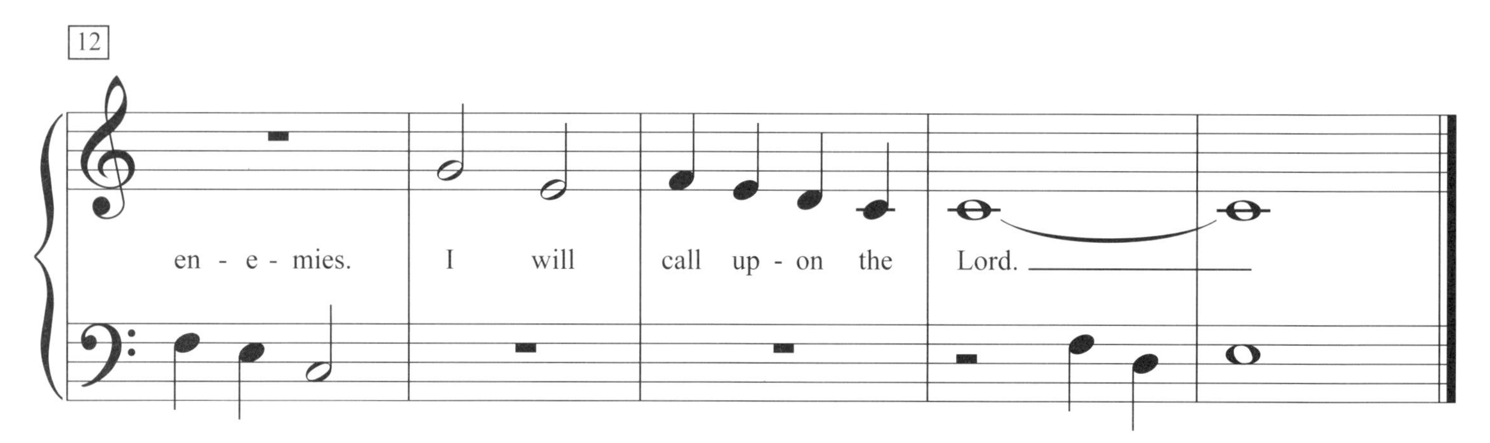

Accompaniment (Student plays one octave higher than written.)

More Precious Than Silver
(Based on Proverbs 3:14–15)
Words and Music by
Lynn DeShazo
Prayerfully ♩ = 112
Note name ____
mp
Lord, You are more precious than silver. Lord, You are more
Note name ____
costly than gold. Lord, You are more beautiful than
diamonds, and nothing I desire compares with You.
Accompaniment (Student plays one octave higher than written.)
Prayerfully ♩ = 112
p

10,000 Reasons

(Bless the Lord)

Words and Music by Jonas Myrin
and Matt Redman

Worshipfully ♩ = 144

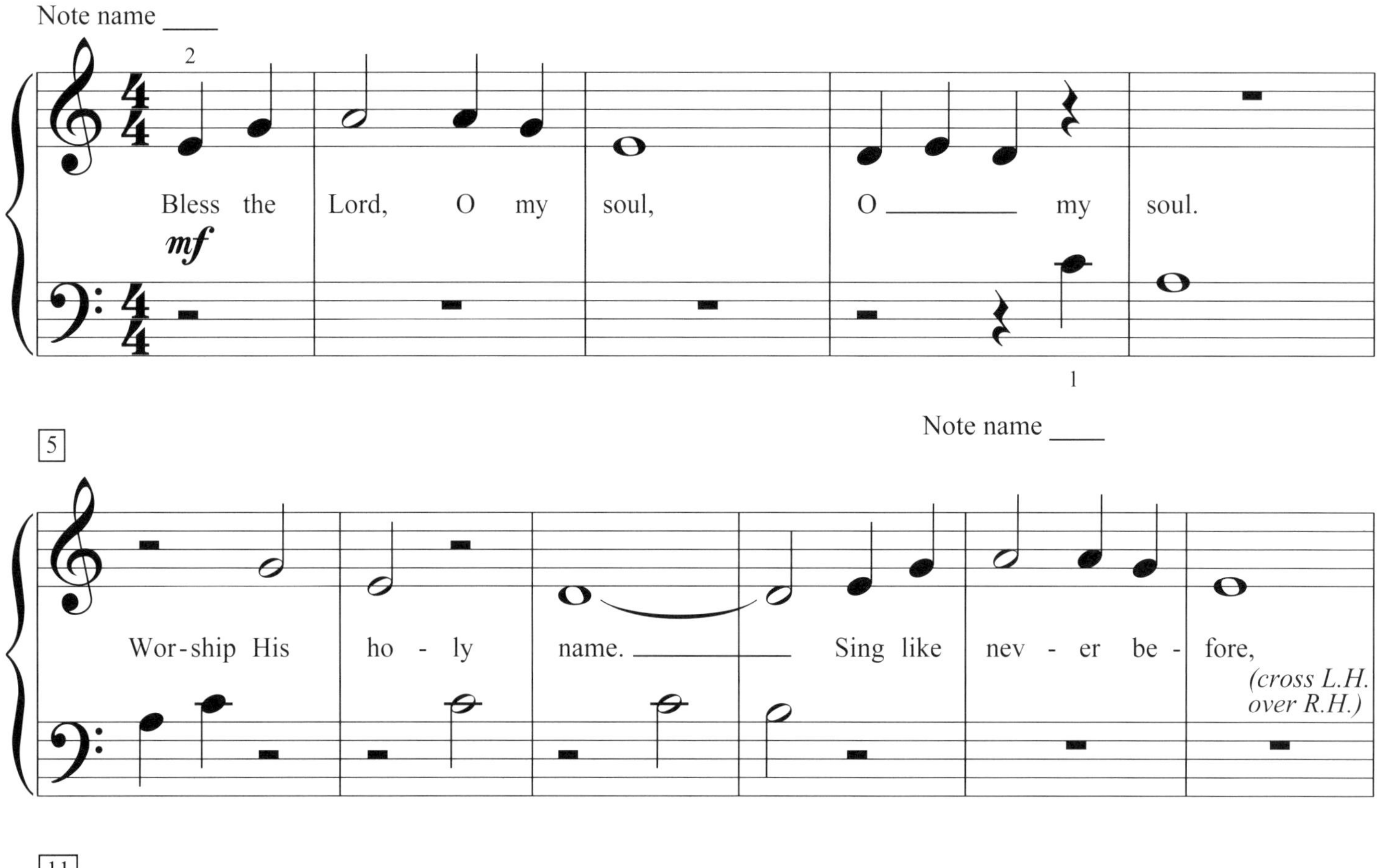

Accompaniment (Student plays one octave higher than written.)

Spirit of the Living God

Words and Music by
Daniel Iverson

All Because of Jesus

Words and Music by
Steve Fee

Christ Is Risen
Words and Music by Mia Fieldes
and Matt Maher
Joyfully ♩ = 160
Note name ____
1
Christ is
mf
ris - en from the dead, tram - pling
ris - en from the dead, we are
1
3
Note name ____
o - ver death by death. Come a - wake, come a -
one with Him a - gain. Come a - wake, come a -
6
1.
wake, come and rise up from the grave. Christ is
wake, come and
9
2.
rise up from the grave.

Offering

Words and Music by
Paul Baloche

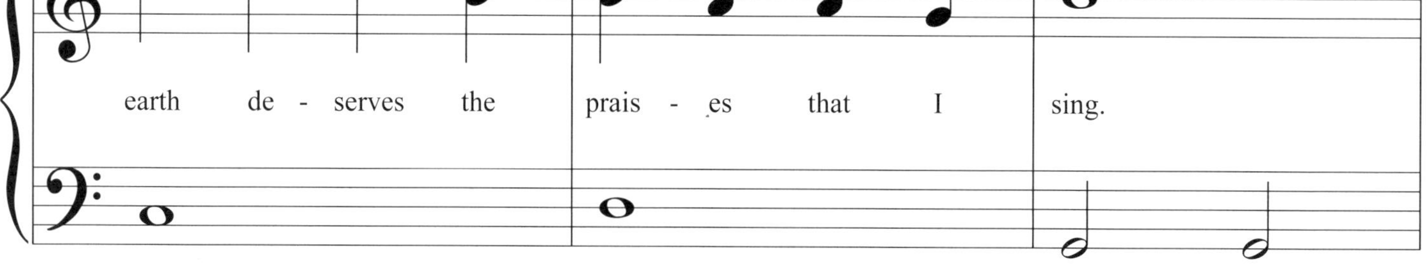

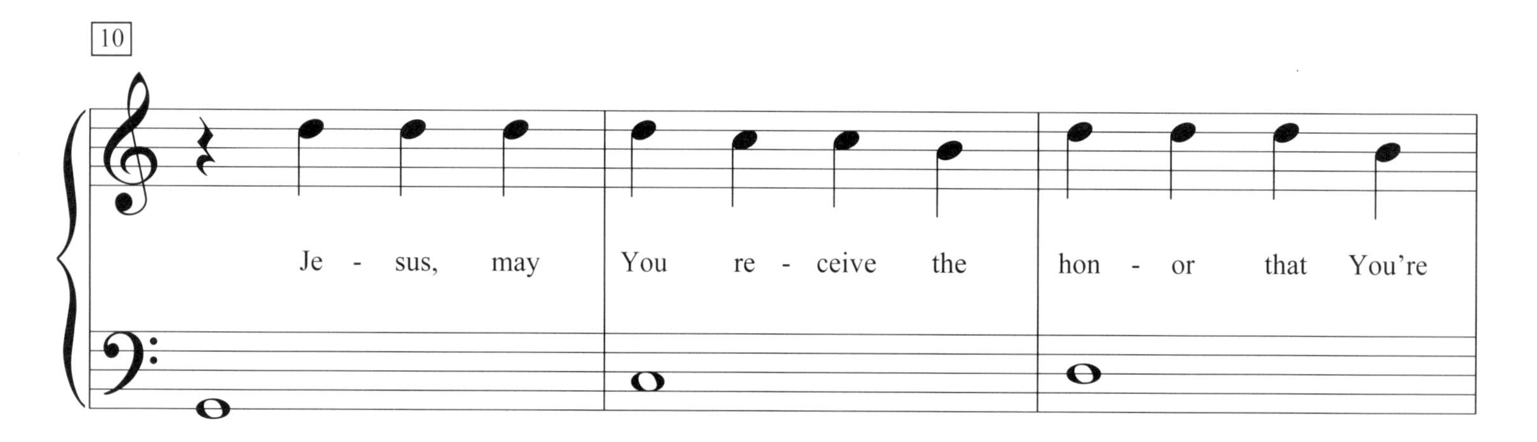

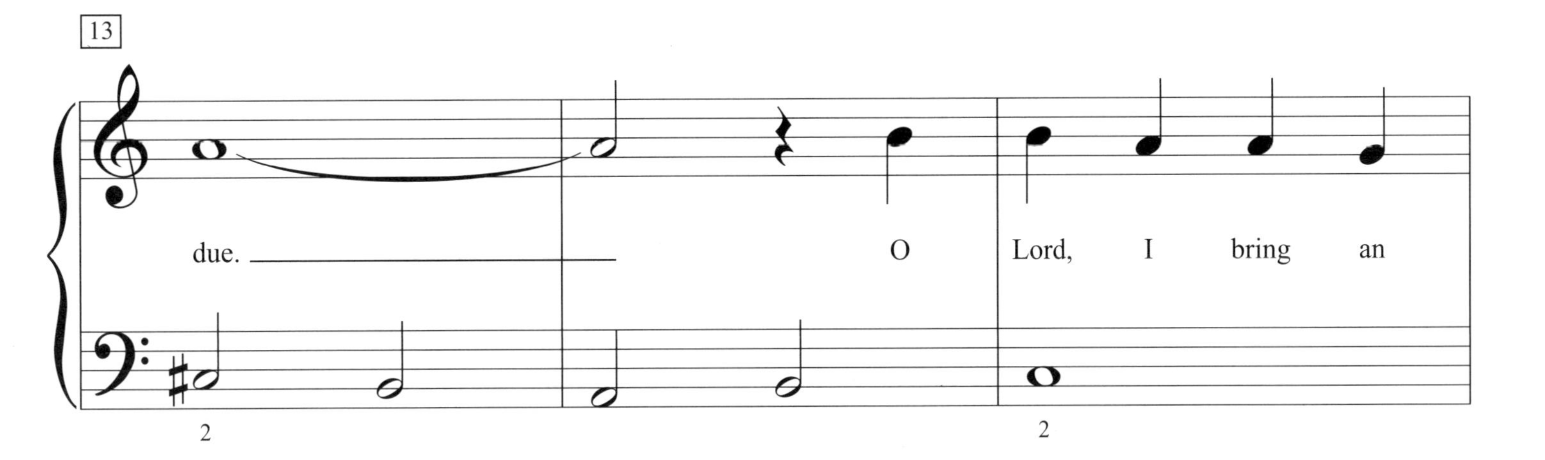

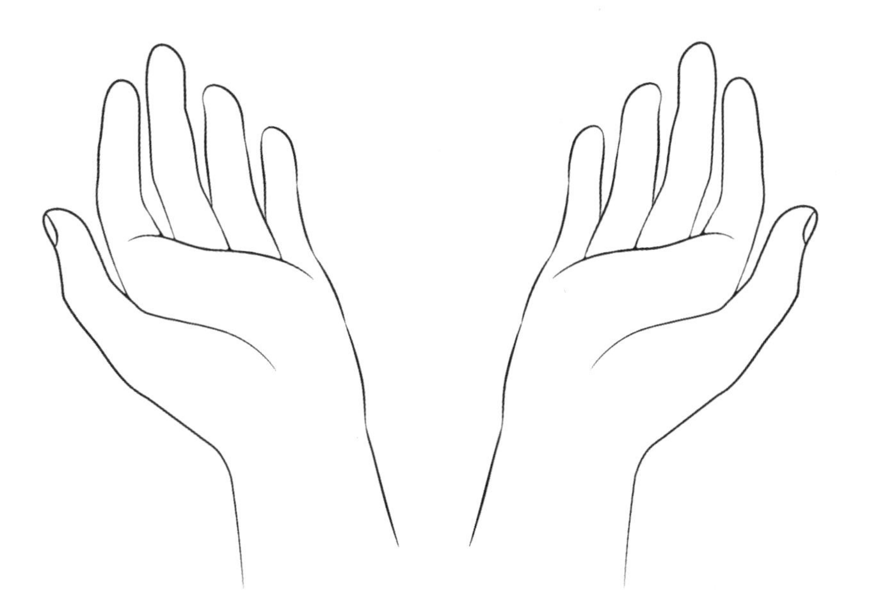

"So brothers and sisters, since God has shown us great mercy, I beg you to offer your lives as a living sacrifice to Him. Your offering must be for God and pleasing to Him, which is the spiritual way for you to worship."
– Romans 12:1, NCV

Your Grace Is Enough

Words and Music by
Matt Maher

13
grace is e - nough for
me,

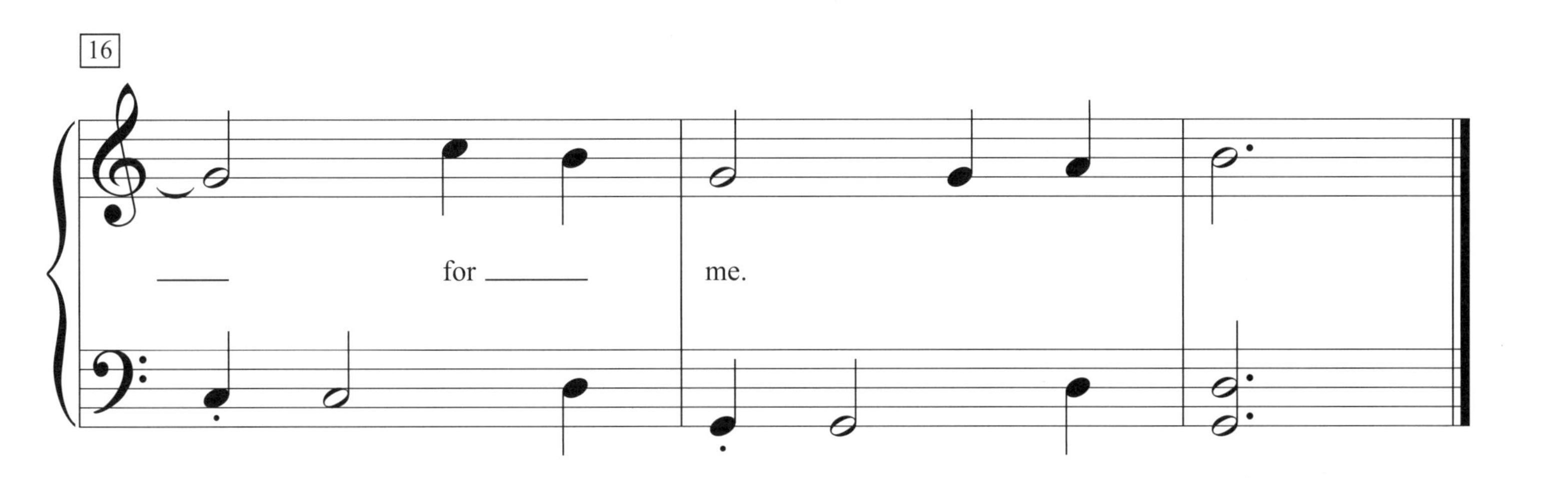
16
for
me.

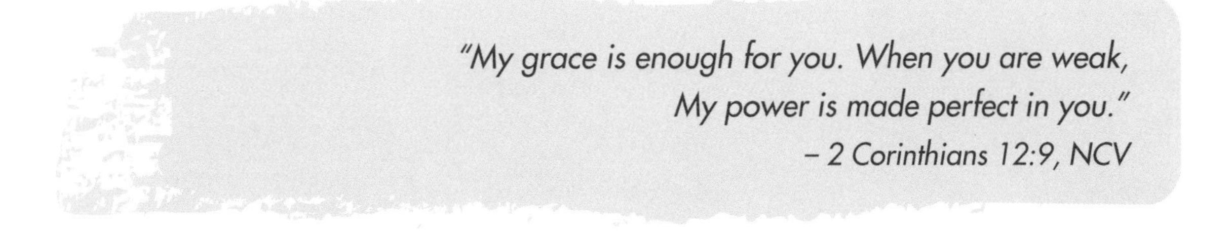
"My grace is enough for you. When you are weak,
My power is made perfect in you."
– 2 Corinthians 12:9, NCV

The BEST Easy Worship Songbooks

For More Information, See Your Local Music Dealer, Or Write To:

HAL•LEONARD® CORPORATION

7777 W. Bluemound Rd. P.O. Box 13819 Milwaukee, WI 53213

www.halleonard.com

Prices, contents, and availability subject to change without notice.

THE BEST PRAISE & WORSHIP SONGS EVER

74 all-time favorites: Awesome God • Breathe • Days of Elijah • Here I Am to Worship • I Could Sing of Your Love Forever • Open the Eyes of My Heart • Shout to the Lord • We Bow Down • dozens more.

00311312 P/V/G....................................$19.99

THE BIG-NOTE WORSHIP BOOK

20 worship tunes for beginning players, including: Agnus Dei • Days of Elijah • Everlasting God • Friend of God • Give Us Clean Hands • Here I Am to Worship • Mighty to Save • Open the Eyes of My Heart • Sing to the King • and more.

00311875 Big-Note Piano........................$10.99

CONTEMPORARY WORSHIP FAVORITES

The Phillip Keveren Series

Easy arrangements of 15 powerful Christian favorites: Beautiful One • Better Is One Day • Breathe • Friend of God • Grace Flows Down • I Give You My Heart • Indescribable • Once Again • Revelation Song • The Wonderful Cross • and more.

00311805 Easy Piano..............................$12.95

THE EASY WORSHIP FAKE BOOK

This beginning fake book includes over 100 songs, all in the key of "C" with simplified chords. Songs include: Above All • Come, Now Is the Time to Worship • He Is Exalted • Lord, I Lift Your Name on High • You're Worthy of My Praise • and dozens more.

00240265 Melody/Lyrics/Chords $19.95

HERE I AM TO WORSHIP – FOR KIDS

This addition to the WorshipTogether series lets the kids join in on the best modern worship songs. Includes 20 favorites: Awesome God • Breathe • God of Wonders • He Is Exalted • Wonderful Maker • You Are My King (Amazing Love) • and more.

00316098 Easy Piano..............................$14.95

HOW GREAT IS OUR GOD

The Phillip Keveren Series

Keveren's big-note arrangements of 15 praise & worship favorites: Above All • Awesome God • Days of Elijah • Forever • Give Thanks • Here I Am to Worship • The Potter's Hand • Shout to the Lord • We Fall Down • more.

00311402 Big-Note Piano........................$12.95

MODERN HYMNS

Easy piano arrangements of 20 contemporary worship favorites: Amazing Grace (My Chains Are Gone) • Before the Throne of God Above • How Deep the Father's Love for Us • In Christ Alone • Take My Life • The Wonderful Cross • and more.

00311859 Easy Piano..............................$12.99

MORE OF THE BEST PRAISE & WORSHIP SONGS EVER

Simplified arrangements of 80 more contemporary worship favorites, including: Beautiful One • Everlasting God • Friend of God • Hear Our Praises • In Christ Alone • The Power of Your Love • Your Grace Is Enough • Your Name • and more.

00311801 Easy Piano..............................$19.99

MY FIRST WORSHIP BOOK

Beginning pianists will love the five-finger piano format used in this songbook featuring eight worship favorites: Friend of God • Give Thanks • Here I Am to Worship • I Will Call Upon the Lord • More Precious Than Silver • Sing to the King • We Fall Down • and more.

00311874 Five-Finger Piano $7.99

PRAISE & WORSHIP FAVORITES

8 arrangements that even beginners can enjoy, including: Ancient of Days • Breathe • Change My Heart Oh God • Come, Now Is the Time to Worship • Here I Am to Worship • Open the Eyes of My Heart • Shine, Jesus, Shine • There Is None like You.

00311271 Beginning Piano Solo $9.95

TIMELESS PRAISE

The Phillip Keveren Series

20 songs of worship wonderfully arranged for easy piano by Phillip Keveren: As the Deer • El Shaddai • Give Thanks • How Beautiful • How Majestic Is Your Name • Lord, I Lift Your Name on High • Shine, Jesus, Shine • There Is a Redeemer • Thy Word • and more.

00310712 Easy Piano..............................$12.95

TODAY'S WORSHIP HITS

16 modern worship favorites, including: Amazed • Beautiful One • Days of Elijah • How Great Is Our God • Sing to the King • and more.

00311439 Easy Piano..............................$10.99

WORSHIP FAVORITES

20 powerful songs arranged for big-note piano: Above All • Forever • Here I Am to Worship • Open the Eyes of My Heart • Shout to the Lord • and dozens more.

00311207 Big-Note Piano........................$10.95

WORSHIP TOGETHER FAVORITES FOR KIDS

This folio features 12 easy arrangements of today's most popular worship songs: Enough • Everlasting God • Forever • How Great Is Our God • Made to Worship • Mountain of God • Wholly Yours • The Wonderful Cross • Yes You Have • You Never Let Go • and more.

00316109 Easy Piano..............................$12.95